W0099655

Benjamin Franklin

Jez Uden

Series Editor **Rob Waring**

Level 3 - ⑤

Benjamin Franklin

Jez Uden

© 2017 Seed Learning, Inc.

Series Editor: Rob Waring
Acquisitions Editor: Liana Robinson
Copy Editor: Casey Malarcher
Cover/Interior Design: Andy Roh

ISBN: 978-1-9464-5225-2

10 9 8 7 6 5 4 3 2 1
21 20 19 18 17

Contents

Benjamin Franklin

Imagine only spending two years in school and going on to become one of the most important people in your country. Well, that is exactly what Benjamin Franklin did!

Benjamin Franklin

He became famous for his clever ideas, his scientific discoveries, and his many inventions. But most of all, he is remembered today for helping to free America from British rule and giving America its independence!

In this book, you'll discover how Franklin helped America gain the stars and stripes.

Early Life

Benjamin Franklin was born in 1706 in Boston, Massachusetts. His family was very poor, and Franklin didn't go to school for very long. He left school to work with his father in their candle shop. Leaving school, however, did not stop him from getting an education.

Massachusetts, America, 1700s

Massachusetts, America, today

Reading and Writing

Franklin learned a lot from reading books. He loved to read anything he could find! Books were Franklin's school.

Franklin loved reading and writing from a very young age.

Franklin also loved to write. He had a very interesting method of improving his own writing. When he finished reading something, he would try to remember it and rewrite it all from memory!

Benjamin Franklin

Antique pen and paper

6

Making the World Better

Franklin was determined to improve the world around him. If something could be done, Franklin wanted to find a way to do it better. This even included his own lifestyle. For

The 8th virtue: justice

example, he once read that a vegetarian diet was healthier than eating meat, so he stopped eating meat.

Franklin also wanted to be seen as a good example to society. He made a list of thirteen good habits, or "virtues"

The 10th virtue: cleanliness

that helped to improve his way of life. He focused on one of them each week until he was good at them all.

Industry: Lose no time; be always employed in something useful; cut off all unnecessary actions

Franklin's 6th virtue from his list of 13 good habits

7

The Junto

Franklin loved to share ideas with others, so he started a discussion group. This group met every week to talk about their ideas and discuss ways of improving the society they lived in. This group was called the Junto.

A funny quote from *Poor Richard's Almanack*

Franklin wrote many of his new ideas in a magazine that he called *Poor Richard's Almanack*. This magazine became very popular, and Franklin soon became famous in America as well as other countries.

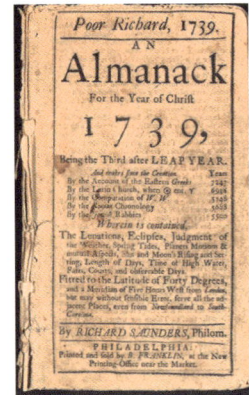

A quote often used today from *Poor Richard's Almanack*

America's First Newspaper

At the age of just 23, Franklin published America's first national newspaper called *The Pennsylvania Gazette.*

Just two years later in 1731, Franklin started America's first public library. This was a huge success. Franklin even said that reading books made Americans smarter!

A political cartoon that appeared in *The Pennsylvania Gazette,* 1754

America's first public library, Pennsylvania

Local Services

Franklin organized the first trained fire department in Philadelphia. He also helped start a police patrol around the city. This helped to keep the streets safe at night.

Certification for a fire company in Pennsylvania

Franklin helped raise money to build the first hospital in America. He also began a school, now known as the University of Pennsylvania.

Pennsylvania Hospital

Franklin's Inventions

What about Franklin's inventions? Franklin invented many useful things, some of which can still be seen today.

Have you ever seen the fins that divers wear on their feet? Franklin had the idea to make fins when he was just a young boy! Today fins are made of rubber. Franklin made his fins from wood!

Swimming fins used by divers

Franklin's eyesight wasn't very good. He needed one pair of glasses to help him read close up and another pair of glasses to see things far away.

Franklin decided to put the two types of glasses together to make one pair. Today they are known as bifocals.

Benjamin Franklin reading

Other inventions included the Franklin stove, which improved the heating systems in houses by producing more heat and less smoke.

The Franklin stove for heating houses

He made improvements to street lamps, so the streets would stay lit for longer.

He even invented a musical instrument he called the glass armonica. It was used by the best musicians around! However, this strange looking instrument is not common today.

Franklin in his study thinking of his experiments

The glass armonica

Electricity

Franklin really enjoyed experimenting with electricity.

One day he attached some metal to a kite and flew it into a lightning storm. The kite attracted the lightning and proved that lightning was an electrical charge. This gave Franklin the idea for his favorite invention—the "lightning rod."

Franklin studying electricity

Lightning rods are metal poles placed on the top of

buildings to protect them from lightning. We still use lightning rods to protect many of our buildings today.

Franklin's kite attracting lightning!

Independence Day

Signing the Declaration of Independence

Benjamin Franklin died in 1790 at the age of 84. And it was during his final years that Franklin helped to change America forever!

At that time, America was ruled by Britain. However, the Americans wanted to be free. So in 1775, America and Britain went to war. On July 4th, 1776, Franklin and other memebers of congress approved the "Declaration of Independence," and just a few years later, America was free.

The Battle of Bunker Hill, 1775

The First American

In 1789, Franklin and the others signed the Constitution of the United States of America. This important document contains the laws about how the country is organized and run. The constitution is still very important today.

The 50 stars represent the 50 states of the USA, and the 13 stripes represent the 13 British colonies that declared independence.

Many people today call Franklin "the First American." And every year on the 4th of July, Americans celebrate Independence Day.

The Declaration of Independence

16

Benjamin Franklin was one of the most popular and inventive leaders in American history. In fact, Americans can see him every day as his face is on the $100 bill. Casually, it is called a Benjamin.

Does your country have a person like Benjamin Franklin?

Comprehension Questions

1. Benjamin Franklin…
   (a) went to university.
   (b) had a limited school education.
   (c) never went to school.
   (d) didn't read much.

2. Franklin loved to…
   (a) travel and hike.
   (b) read and write.
   (c) swim and play tennis.
   (d) sleep and cook.

3. Franklin wanted to be…
   (a) a handsome actor.
   (b) a powerful business owner.
   (c) a rich and famous land owner.
   (d) an example to society.

4. The Junto was…
   (a) a discussion group.
   (b) a newspaper.
   (c) a gazette.
   (d) a magazine.

5. Franklin was the first to…
   (a) raise money for a hospital.
   (b) open a public library.
   (c) organize police patrols.
   (d) All of the above

6. Franklin invented…
   (a) something for swimming.
   (b) special eyeglasses.
   (c) a heater.
   (d) All of the above

7. Franklin was…
   (a) a scientist.
   (b) a writer.
   (c) a publisher.
   (d) All of the above

8. Franklin did experiments with…
   (a) wind.
   (b) gas.
   (c) electricity.
   (d) All of the above

9. He signed the…
   (a) Statement of Independence.
   (b) Document of Independence.
   (c) Treaty of Independence.
   (d) Declaration of Independence.

10. His face appears…
    (a) on a kite.
    (b) on the US flag.
    (c) on money.
    (d) on TV.

Glossary

- **approve** to say yes to or allow something

- **congress** an elected group of representatives who make the laws in some countries

- **constitution** a set of laws for a country

- **contain** to have

- **document** a paper with official information on it

- **gazette** a type of newspaper

- **declaration** an official statement

- **independence** the state of being free from control

- **invent** to create something new for the first time

- **invention** something that is created for the first time

- **kite** a thin device flown in the wind on string

- **lifestyle** the way that a person lives their life

- **lightning** a flash of electricity generated between clouds or a cloud and the ground during a storm

- **member** a person who belongs to a group

- **society** the group of people who live in the same community or under the same law

- **stove** something that you cook food on or heat a room with

- **street lamp** a light on a tall post next to a street

- **vegetarian** not eating or having any meat

- **virtue** a good quality in someone's personality

World History Timeline

This chart shows a rough overview of world history.
Some of the dates have been simplified.

World History Timeline

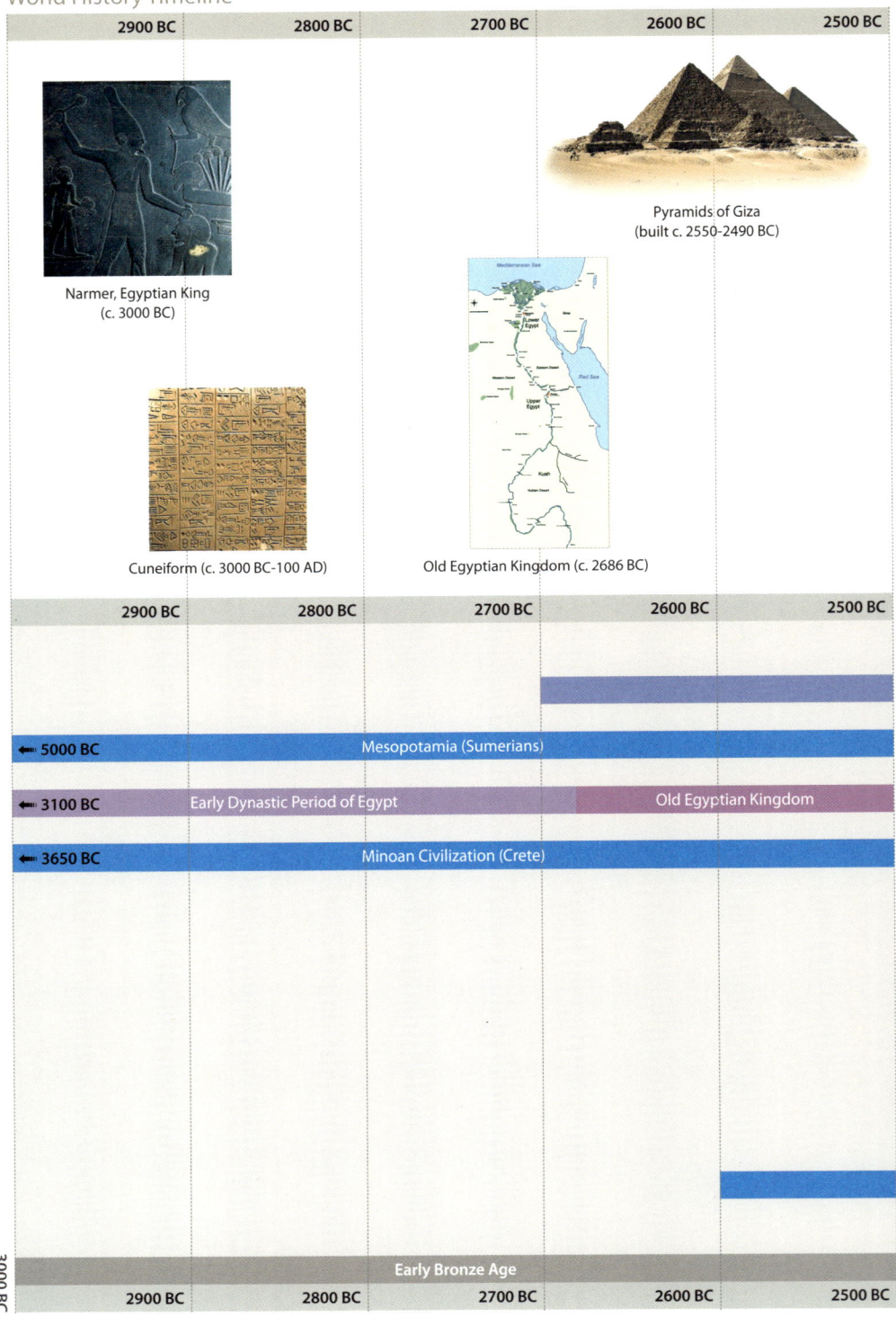

| 2900 BC | 2800 BC | 2700 BC | 2600 BC | 2500 BC |

Narmer, Egyptian King
(c. 3000 BC)

Pyramids of Giza
(built c. 2550-2490 BC)

Cuneiform (c. 3000 BC-100 AD)

Old Egyptian Kingdom (c. 2686 BC)

| 2900 BC | 2800 BC | 2700 BC | 2600 BC | 2500 BC |

◀ 5000 BC Mesopotamia (Sumerians)

◀ 3100 BC Early Dynastic Period of Egypt   Old Egyptian Kingdom

◀ 3650 BC Minoan Civilization (Crete)

Early Bronze Age

| 2900 BC | 2800 BC | 2700 BC | 2600 BC | 2500 BC |

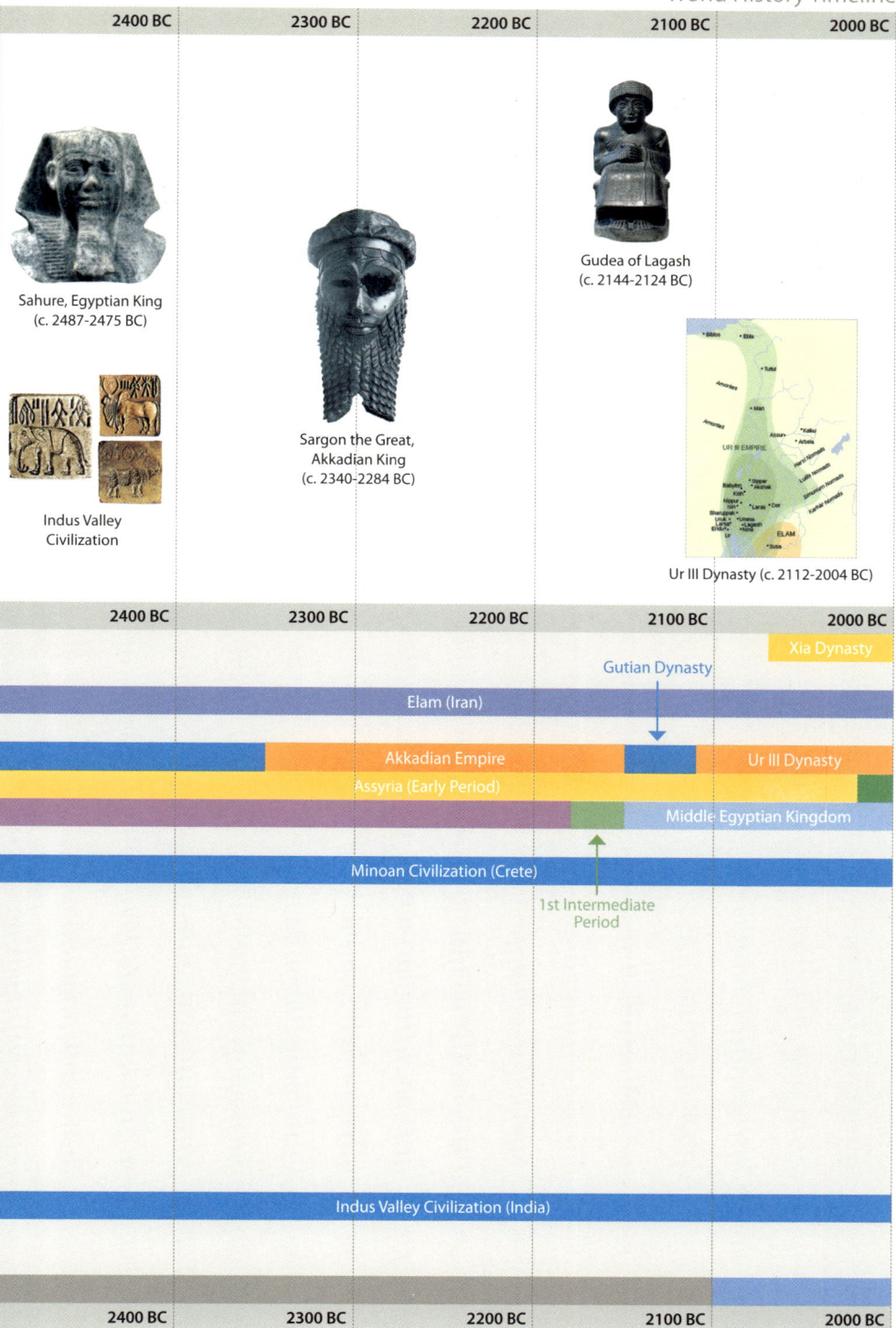

World History Timeline

2400 BC	2300 BC	2200 BC	2100 BC	2000 BC

Sahure, Egyptian King
(c. 2487-2475 BC)

Indus Valley
Civilization

Sargon the Great,
Akkadian King
(c. 2340-2284 BC)

Gudea of Lagash
(c. 2144-2124 BC)

Ur III Dynasty (c. 2112-2004 BC)

2400 BC	2300 BC	2200 BC	2100 BC	2000 BC

Xia Dynasty

Gutian Dynasty

Elam (Iran)

Akkadian Empire

Ur III Dynasty

Assyria (Early Period)

Middle Egyptian Kingdom

Minoan Civilization (Crete)

1st Intermediate
Period

Indus Valley Civilization (India)

2400 BC	2300 BC	2200 BC	2100 BC	2000 BC

World History Timeline

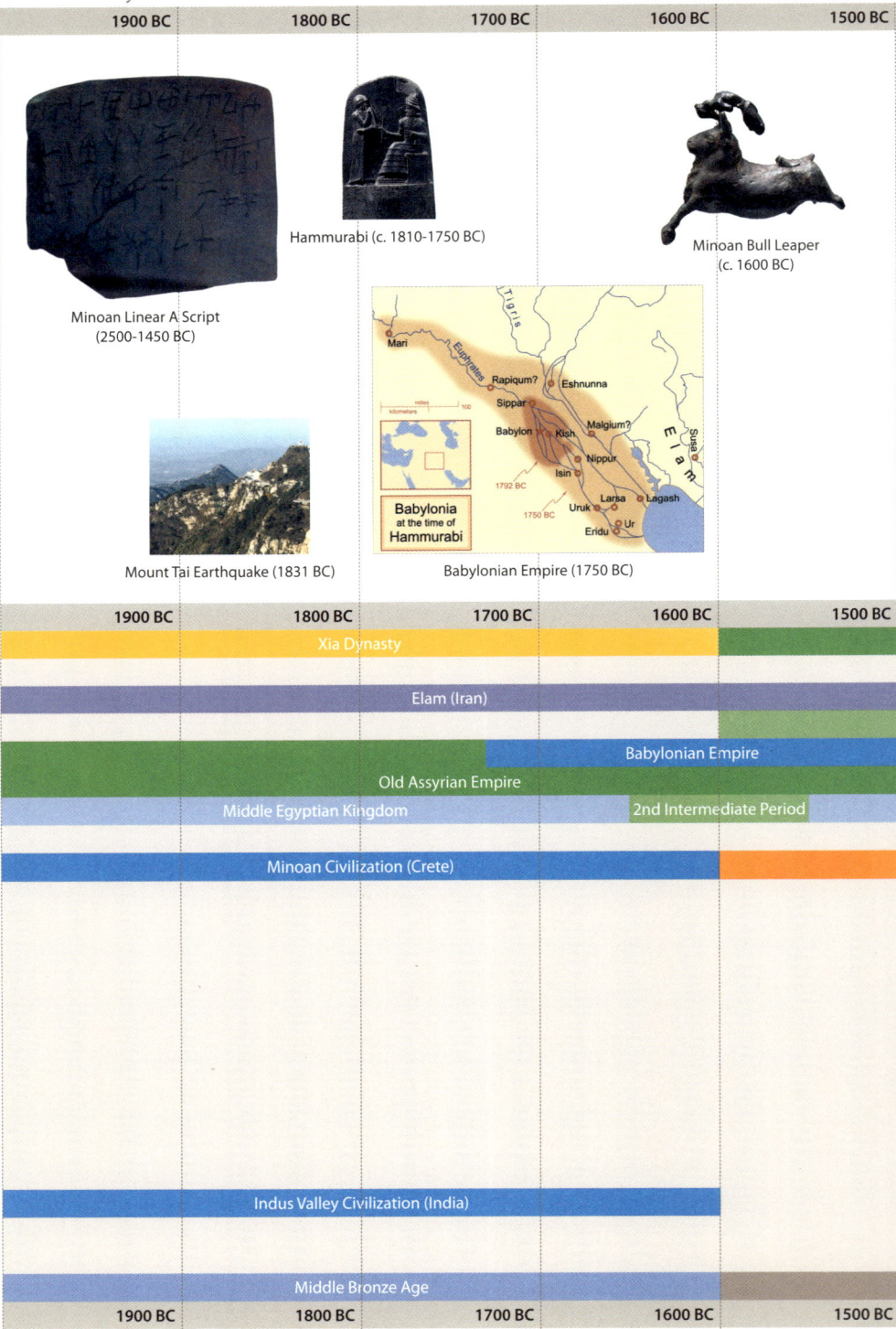

1900 BC	1800 BC	1700 BC	1600 BC	1500 BC

Minoan Linear A Script
(2500-1450 BC)

Hammurabi (c. 1810-1750 BC)

Minoan Bull Leaper
(c. 1600 BC)

Mount Tai Earthquake (1831 BC)

Babylonia at the time of Hammurabi

Babylonian Empire (1750 BC)

1900 BC	1800 BC	1700 BC	1600 BC	1500 BC

Xia Dynasty

Elam (Iran)

Babylonian Empire

Old Assyrian Empire

Middle Egyptian Kingdom

2nd Intermediate Period

Minoan Civilization (Crete)

Indus Valley Civilization (India)

Middle Bronze Age

1900 BC	1800 BC	1700 BC	1600 BC	1500 BC

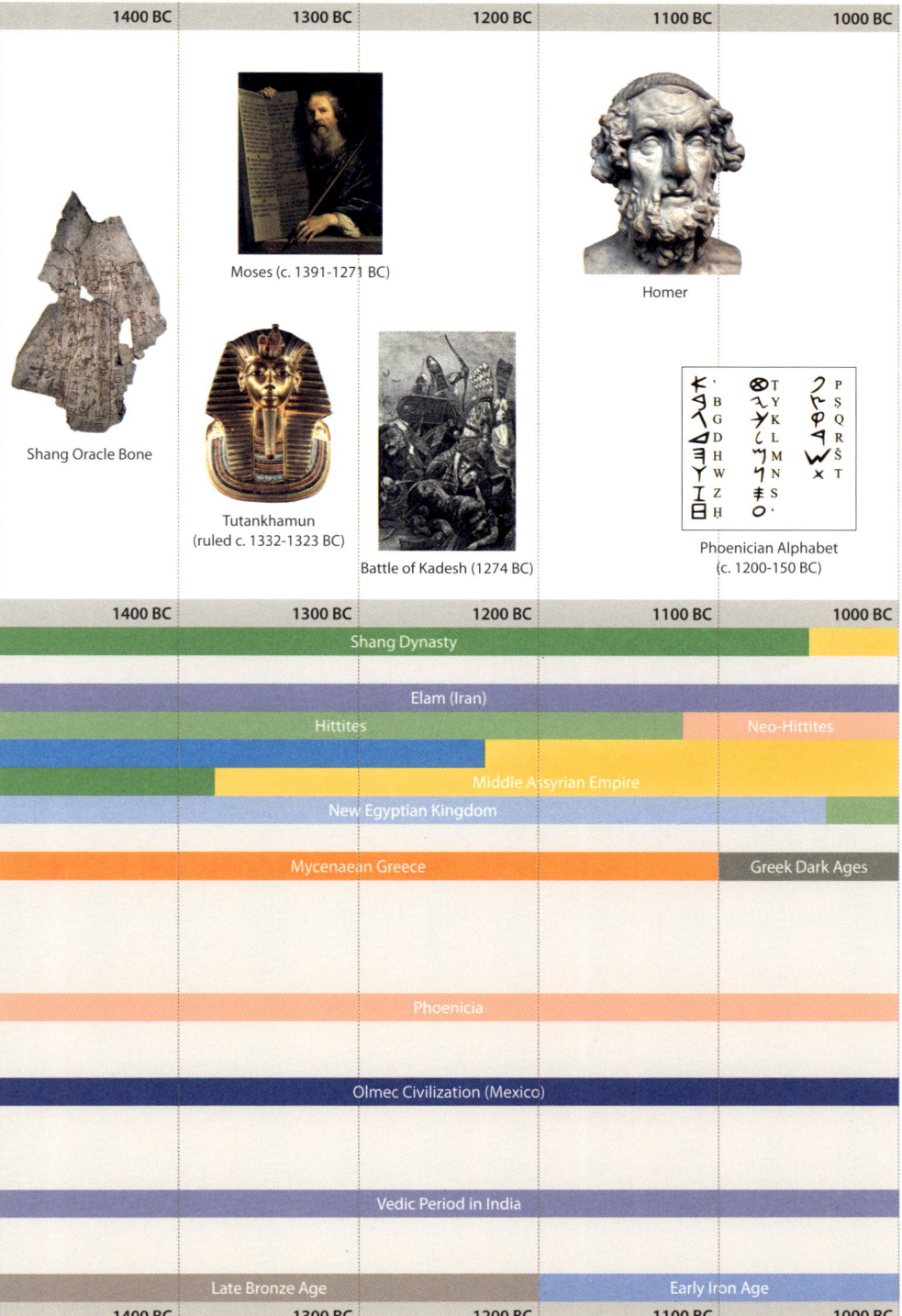

1400 BC	1300 BC	1200 BC	1100 BC	1000 BC

Moses (c. 1391-1271 BC)

Homer

Shang Oracle Bone

Tutankhamun
(ruled c. 1332-1323 BC)

Battle of Kadesh (1274 BC)

Phoenician Alphabet
(c. 1200-150 BC)

1400 BC	1300 BC	1200 BC	1100 BC	1000 BC

Shang Dynasty

Elam (Iran)

Hittites · Neo-Hittites

Middle Assyrian Empire

New Egyptian Kingdom

Mycenaean Greece · Greek Dark Ages

Phoenicia

Olmec Civilization (Mexico)

Vedic Period in India

Late Bronze Age · Early Iron Age

1400 BC	1300 BC	1200 BC	1100 BC	1000 BC

World History Timeline

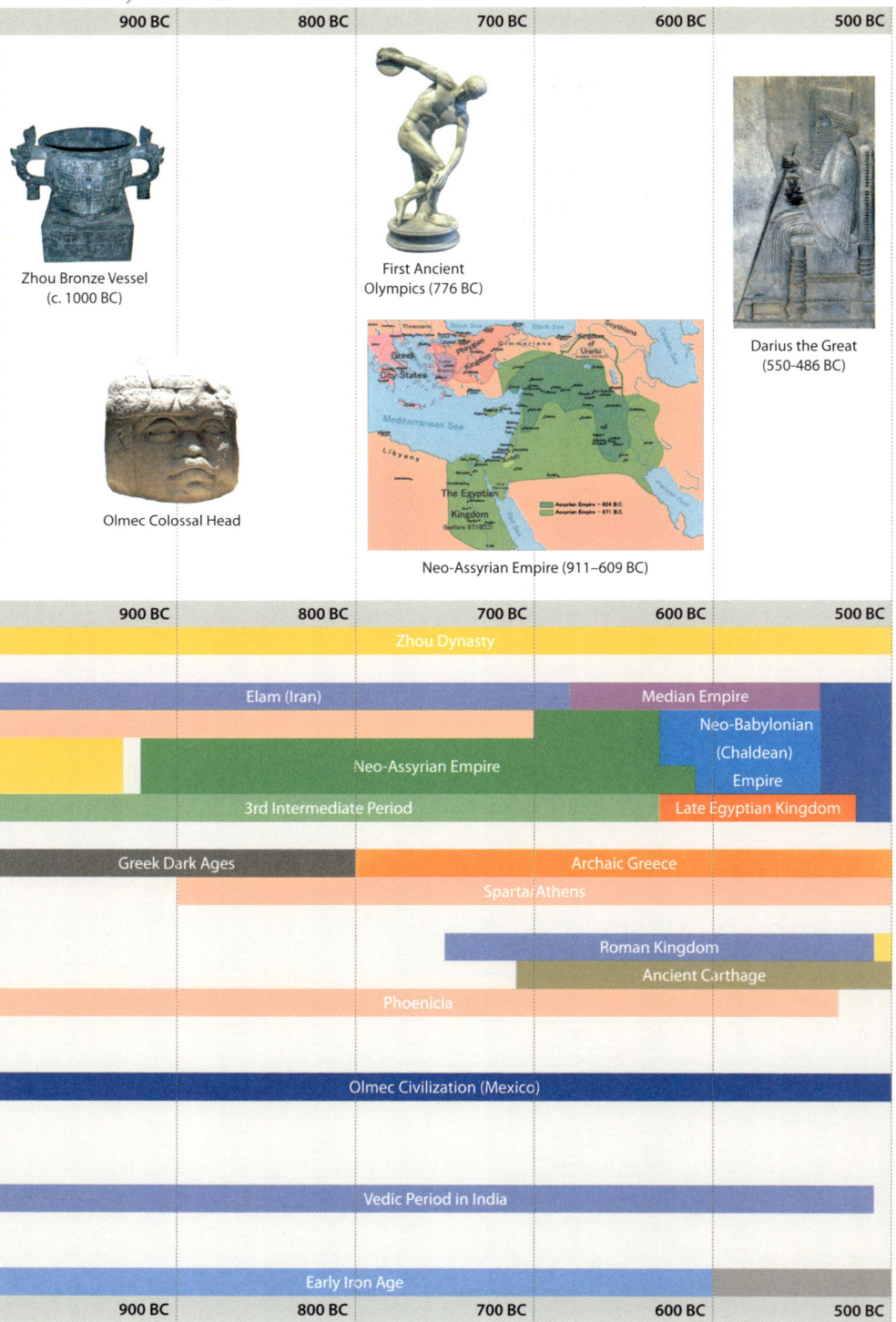

900 BC	800 BC	700 BC	600 BC	500 BC

Zhou Bronze Vessel
(c. 1000 BC)

First Ancient
Olympics (776 BC)

Olmec Colossal Head

Neo-Assyrian Empire (911–609 BC)

Darius the Great
(550-486 BC)

900 BC	800 BC	700 BC	600 BC	500 BC

Zhou Dynasty

Elam (Iran)

Median Empire

Neo-Babylonian
(Chaldean)
Empire

Neo-Assyrian Empire

3rd Intermediate Period

Late Egyptian Kingdom

Greek Dark Ages

Archaic Greece

Sparta/Athens

Roman Kingdom

Ancient Carthage

Phoenicia

Olmec Civilization (Mexico)

Vedic Period in India

Early Iron Age

900 BC	800 BC	700 BC	600 BC	500 BC

| 400 BC | 300 BC | 200 BC | 100 BC | 0 |

Alexander the Great
(356-323 BC)

Hannibal
(247-183 BC)

Julius Caesar
(100-44 BC)

Cleopatra
(69-30 BC)

Battle of Salamis
(480 BC)

Seleucid Empire (312-63 BC)

Rossetta Stone
(created 196 BC)

| 400 BC | 300 BC | 200 BC | 100 BC | 0 |

Zhou Dynasty

Qin

Han Dynasty

Achaemenid (Persian) Empire

Alexander the Great

Parthian Empire

Seleucid Empire

Ptolemaic Kingdom

(Hellenistic Greece)

Classical Greece

Sparta/Athens

Roman Empire

Roman Republic

Roman Empire

Maurya Empire

Middle Iron Age

| 400 BC | 300 BC | 200 BC | 100 BC | 0 |

World History Timeline

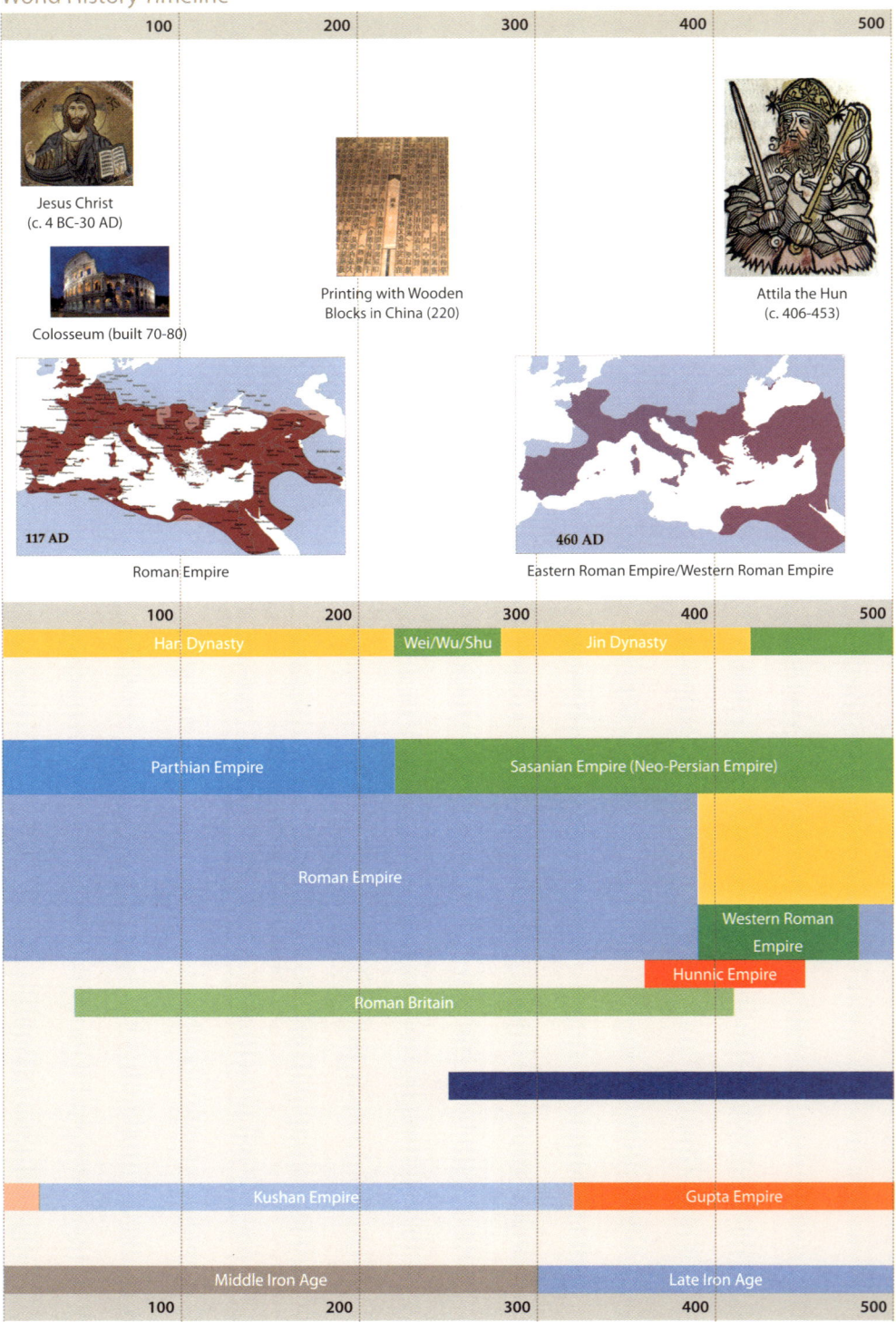

| 100 | 200 | 300 | 400 | 500 |

Jesus Christ
(c. 4 BC-30 AD)

Colosseum (built 70-80)

Printing with Wooden
Blocks in China (220)

Attila the Hun
(c. 406-453)

117 AD

Roman Empire

460 AD

Eastern Roman Empire/Western Roman Empire

| 100 | 200 | 300 | 400 | 500 |

Han Dynasty — Wei/Wu/Shu — Jin Dynasty

Parthian Empire — Sasanian Empire (Neo-Persian Empire)

Roman Empire

Western Roman Empire

Hunnic Empire

Roman Britain

Kushan Empire — Gupta Empire

Middle Iron Age — Late Iron Age

| 100 | 200 | 300 | 400 | 500 |

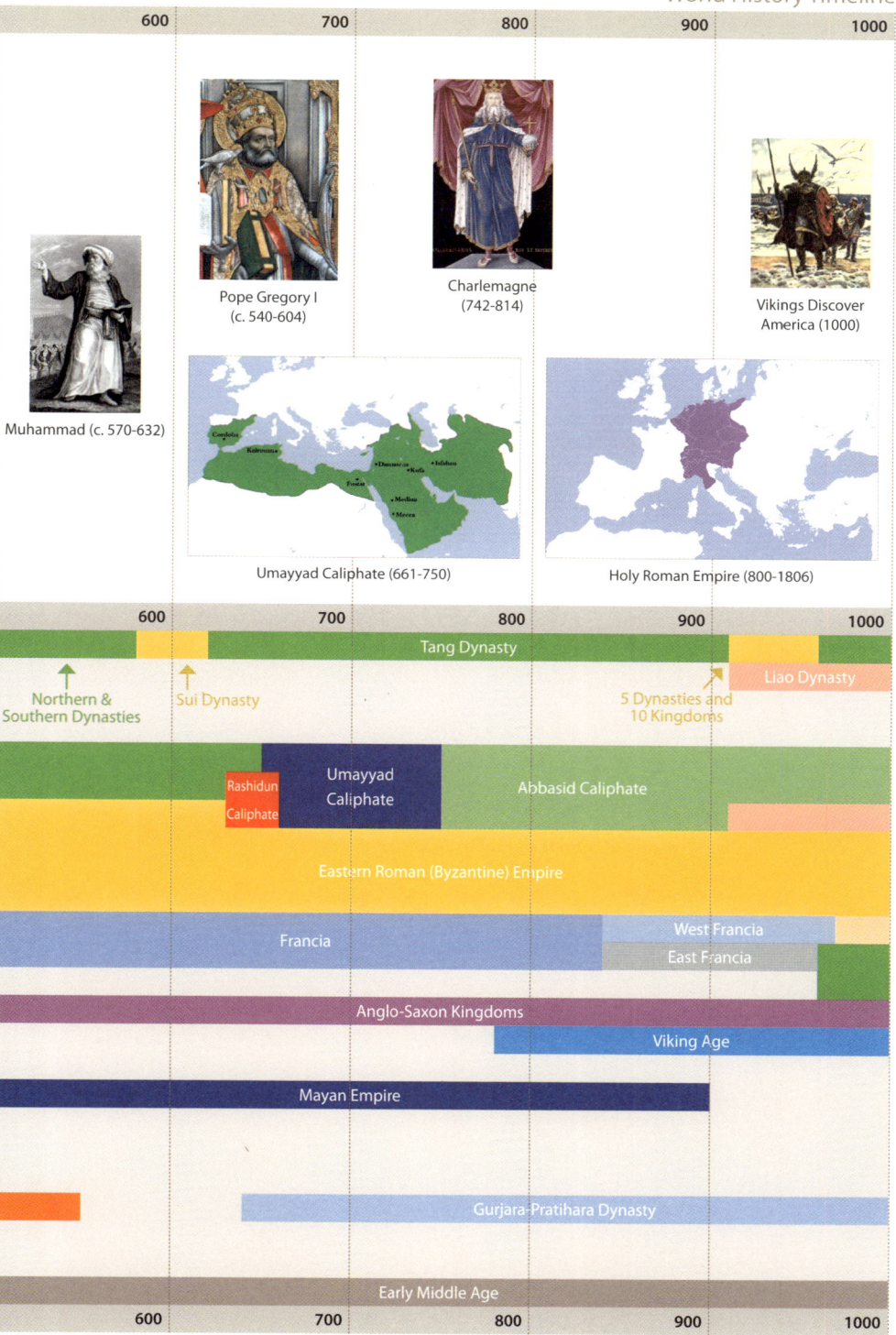

World History Timeline

600   700   800   900   1000

Pope Gregory I
(c. 540-604)

Charlemagne
(742-814)

Vikings Discover
America (1000)

Muhammad (c. 570-632)

Umayyad Caliphate (661-750)

Holy Roman Empire (800-1806)

600   700   800   900   1000

Tang Dynasty

Liao Dynasty

Northern &
Southern Dynasties

Sui Dynasty

5 Dynasties and
10 Kingdoms

Rashidun
Caliphate

Umayyad
Caliphate

Abbasid Caliphate

Eastern Roman (Byzantine) Empire

Francia

West Francia

East Francia

Anglo-Saxon Kingdoms

Viking Age

Mayan Empire

Gurjara-Pratihara Dynasty

Early Middle Age

600   700   800   900   1000

World History Timeline

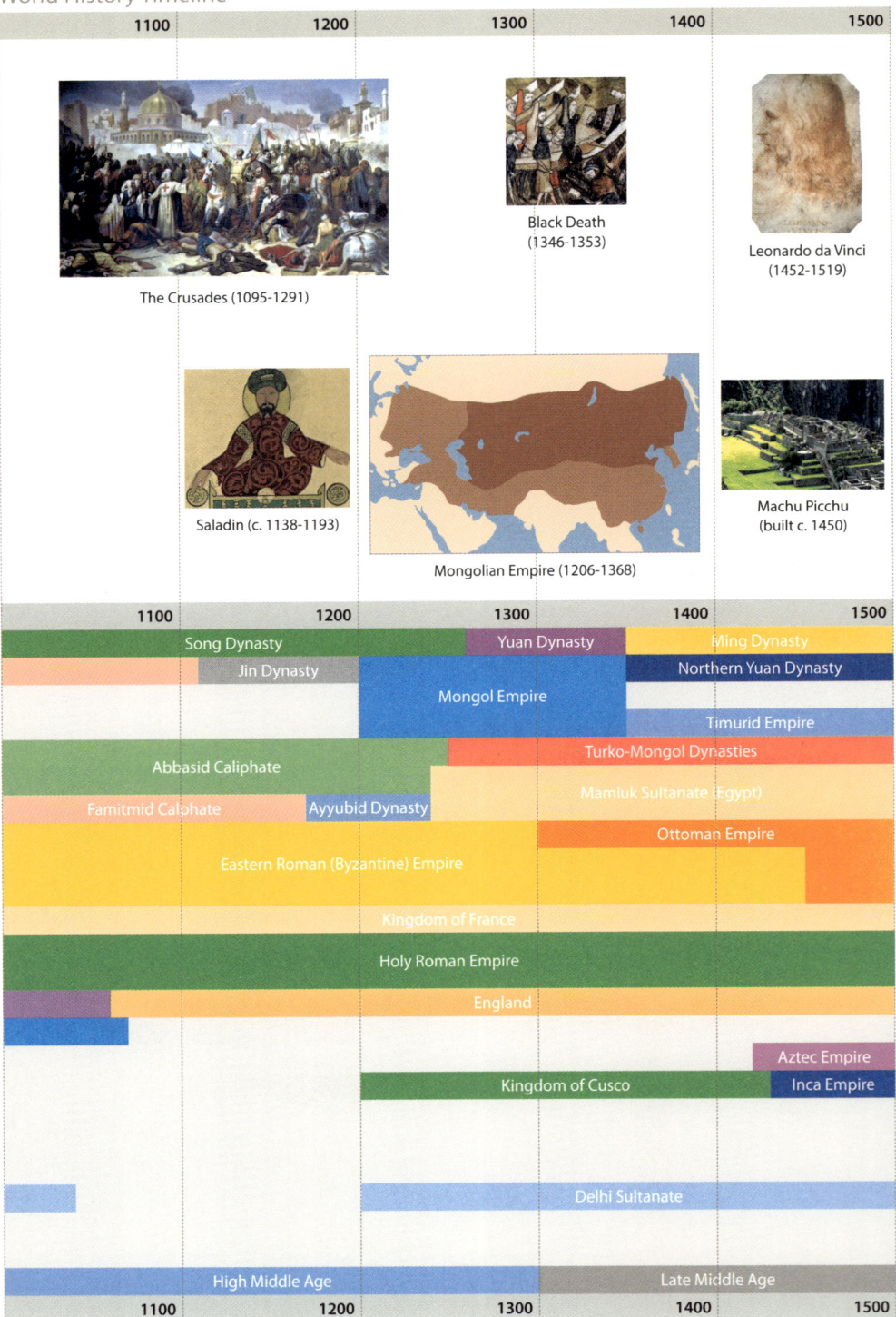

| 1100 | 1200 | 1300 | 1400 | 1500 |

The Crusades (1095-1291)

Black Death (1346-1353)

Leonardo da Vinci (1452-1519)

Saladin (c. 1138-1193)

Mongolian Empire (1206-1368)

Machu Picchu (built c. 1450)

| 1100 | 1200 | 1300 | 1400 | 1500 |

Song Dynasty

Yuan Dynasty

Ming Dynasty

Jin Dynasty

Northern Yuan Dynasty

Mongol Empire

Timurid Empire

Abbasid Caliphate

Turko-Mongol Dynasties

Famitmid Calphate

Ayyubid Dynasty

Mamluk Sultanate (Egypt)

Ottoman Empire

Eastern Roman (Byzantine) Empire

Kingdom of France

Holy Roman Empire

England

Aztec Empire

Kingdom of Cusco

Inca Empire

Delhi Sultanate

High Middle Age

Late Middle Age

| 1100 | 1200 | 1300 | 1400 | 1500 |

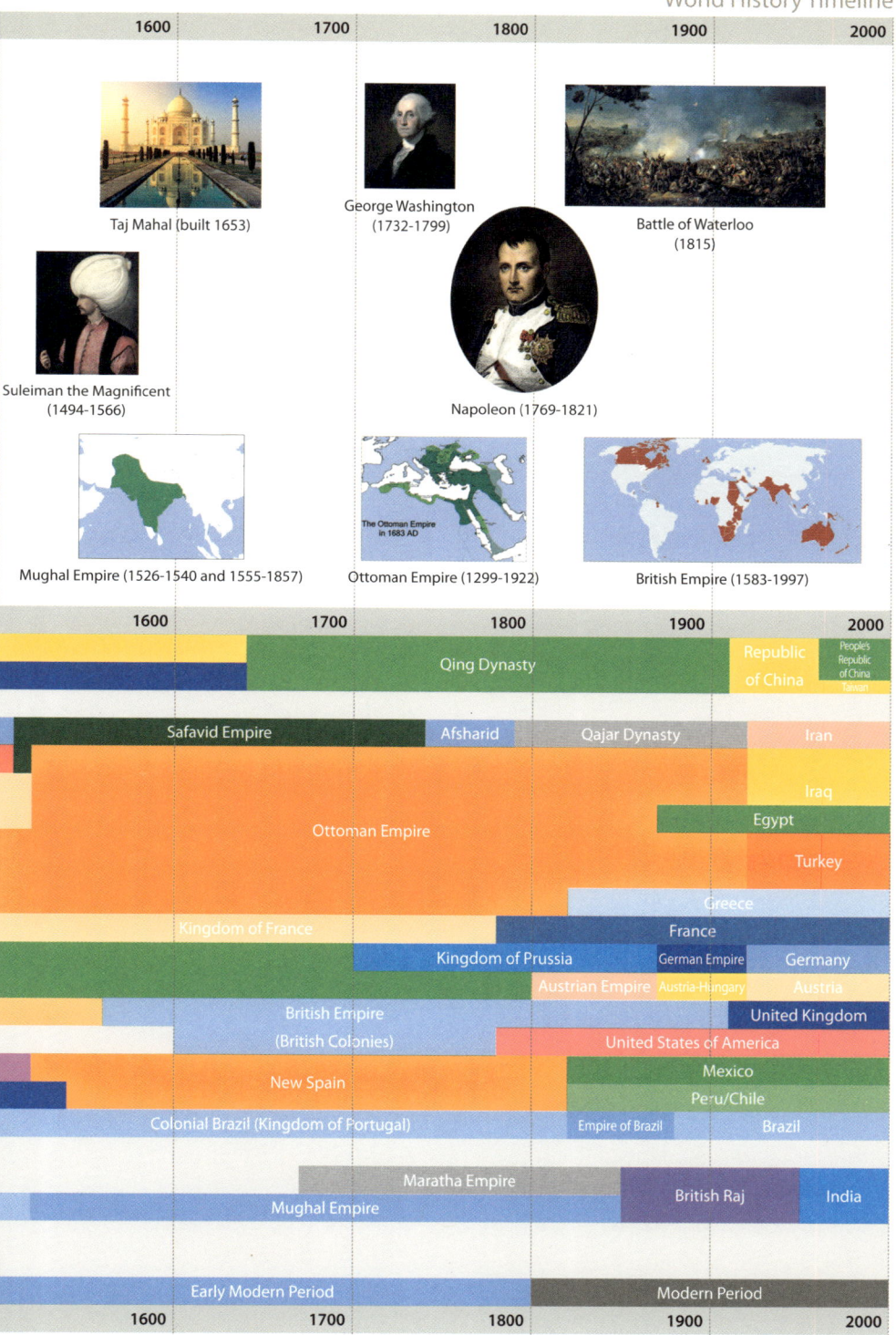

World History Timeline

| 1600 | 1700 | 1800 | 1900 | 2000 |

Taj Mahal (built 1653)

George Washington
(1732-1799)

Battle of Waterloo
(1815)

Suleiman the Magnificent
(1494-1566)

Napoleon (1769-1821)

The Ottoman Empire
in 1683 AD

Mughal Empire (1526-1540 and 1555-1857)

Ottoman Empire (1299-1922)

British Empire (1583-1997)

| 1600 | 1700 | 1800 | 1900 | 2000 |

Qing Dynasty

Republic of China

People's Republic of China

Taiwan

Safavid Empire

Afsharid

Qajar Dynasty

Iran

Iraq

Ottoman Empire

Egypt

Turkey

Greece

Kingdom of France

France

Kingdom of Prussia

German Empire

Germany

Austrian Empire

Austria-Hungary

Austria

British Empire
(British Colonies)

United Kingdom

United States of America

New Spain

Mexico

Peru/Chile

Colonial Brazil (Kingdom of Portugal)

Empire of Brazil

Brazil

Maratha Empire

British Raj

India

Mughal Empire

Early Modern Period

Modern Period

| 1600 | 1700 | 1800 | 1900 | 2000 |

List of Books

LEVEL 1

1. Calendars and the History of Time
2. Searching for El Dorado
3. The Tower of Babel
4. The Pilgrim Fathers
5. Traveling on the Silk Road
6. The Invention of Writing
7. The Making of a United Europe
8. The Magic of Numbers
9. The Persian Empire
10. The Great Wall of China

LEVEL 2

1. The Ottomans and Their Empire
2. The War Between the States
3. The Industrial Revolution
4. The Agricultural Revolution
5. Wars in the Middle East
6. The British Empire, Then and Now
7. The Neo-Assyrian Empire
8. The Rise and Fall of Communism
9. The History of Printing
10. The Vikings and Erik the Red

LEVEL 3

1. Space Exploration
2. The Spanish Conquest of the Americas
3. Cleopatra
4. The French Revolution
5. Benjamin Franklin
6. Galileo Galilei
7. The Battle of Salamis
8. Tea and Wars
9. Christopher Columbus
10. The Trojan War

LEVEL 4

1. Alexander the Great
2. Leonardo da Vinci
3. The Neo-Babylonian Empire
4. The Birth of the United States of America
5. Life and Death in Ancient Egypt
6. Life in the Roman Army
7. The Great Plane Race
8. Genghis Khan
9. Korea: A Land Divided by War
10. The Crusades

LEVEL 5

1. The Story of the Renaissance
2. The Great Plague
3. The Mughal Empire
4. Popes and Kings in the Middle Ages
5. Tutankhamun
6. The Story of the Reformation
7. The Medical Revolution
8. Decisive Battles of World War II
9. China: The New Superpower
10. The Great Depression

LEVEL 6

1. World War I
2. Communication Technology
3. The First Democracies
4. The Cold War
5. Global Trade and Peace
6. Greek Culture
7. Napoleon
8. The History of Transportation
9. Capitalism: Good or Evil?
10. China's First Empire: The Qin Dynasty